Amended:

AMENDED:

A YOUNG BLACK REVELATION

WILL CREAGH

RBH Professional Publishing

Southfield, Michigan

Amended: A Young Black Revelation
Copyright © 2023 by Will Creagh, all rights reserved.

No part of this book may be used or reproduced in any manner whatsoever without written permission from the author.

Published by RBH Professional Publishing, A division of
RBH Professional Development Institute
2000 Town Center Drive, Suite 1900
Southfield, Michigan 48075
(866) 600-6322
www.rbhprofesshionalpublishing.com

Book Cover Illustrator
Justin Lindberg

Library of Congress Cataloging-in-Publication Data
Library of Congress Control Number: 2023908316

ISBN: 978-1-7339533-8-2
eISBN: 978-1-7339533-9-9

Dedication

For my grandma, my cousin Nia, my tee tee Ree, and my grandad….

Contents

	Preface	ix
1.	The Daycare	1
2.	Sam Cooke	7
3.	Playing the Game	11
4.	The Nod	23
5.	They Must See Roaches	31
6.	Stigma	41
7.	Epilogue:	45
	About the Author	51

Amended:

Preface

It rings in my mind as if I am standing there reading it now: "You are standing on a site where enslaved people were warehoused." These are the words one is greeted with when entering EJI's Legacy Museum in Montgomery, Alabama. I visited the museum in Spring 2019 on a civil rights retreat organized by me and others from the Black student union at my alma mater, Wheaton College in Illinois.

As I journeyed through the museum that goes from "slavery to mass incarceration," I learned more than I could have imagined about America's sins toward Black people. At the end of the exhibits, I somberly exited the former slave warehouse—a "free" African American man—onto Coosa Street trying to imagine what I am to take from all I had just digested. Situated on the outer wall of the building was my answer in the moment from the prolific poet, Maya Angelou: "History, despite its wrenching pain, cannot be unlived, but if faced with courage, need not be lived again."

I think back to this day often now, especially in the wake of 2020's history bringing so much more of that "wrenching pain" that Angelou was talking about. In the summer of 2020, I was among the millions of protesters who took to the streets to demand that 400 years of oppression be faced with courage. We were propelled by 8 minutes and 46 seconds of video footage that shows a Black man by the name of George Floyd being murdered. At the same time, a global pandemic due to a virus named COVID-19 was disproportionately affecting Black lives.

The aftermath of such atrocities calls for some kind of change socially, economically, politically. In the wake of slavery and the civil rights movement, there have been amendments politically, specifically in the Constitution, and these seismic changes shifted America's social and economic life as well. Yet, in 2020, the world witnessed the public lynching of a Black man a century and a half after the 13th amendment of the Constitution set him "free."

I live in a constant state of befuddlement as I survey America's history with Black life. Most people have no problem calling slavery an absolutely heinous part of this story; however, a lot seem to argue that the carnage ceased with the 13th and 14th amendments. In the time since the 14th amendment, Black America has experienced sharecropping, the lynching era, Jim Crow, redlining, mass incarceration, and more. One has to think that it is time to ask: What does it mean for your life, your humanity, your livelihood to rest upon a constitutional amendment?

That is the question I hope to explore in this book. We as Black people live an amended life here in the United States of America. This life has tangible affects mentally, physically, socially, economically, and every other -ally that you can think of. I will attempt to tackle this question by perusing my own journey to racial consciousness—or utter bewilderment—as a Black man in America.

WILL CREAGH

1

The Daycare

The world has never seen any people turned loose to such restitution as were the four million slaves of the South…They were free without roofs to cover them, or bread to eat, or land to cultivate, and as a consequence died in such numbers as to awaken the hope of their enemies that they would soon disappear." – Frederick Douglass.

As far as I can remember, my state of confusion started at The Daycare. I was six years old. My grandma was my primary caretaker while my mom was away as a travel nurse. My grandma worked as a preschool teacher and babysitter at a nearby daycare called First Feats Daycare and School. As a matter of fact, all of my immediate family worked there at some point: my auntie Tina, my auntie Ree, my auntie Tracy, my auntie Louis, and my cousin Shara. This was the place where me, my siblings, and all my cousins grew up. It is where we learned our ABCs, how to tie our shoes, and how to play games like "patty cake" and "ring around the rosy."

I remember waking up early on days that my grandmother, or "granny" as I called her, had to open up the daycare. I witnessed her cooking breakfast with the same love and care for about 30 children between the ages of 6 months to 13 years old, in the same manner when she cooked breakfast for me. I watched her and my aunts love-on and discipline these children with the same love and discipline they used to raise me. Throughout my life, my family and I have referred to this formational place as "The Daycare." Everything about "The Daycare" told me that it was ours and that it belonged to my family.

My grandmother and aunts did all the work. They prepared the meals. They did the shopping. They took care of the children. They cleaned the building. Despite all of this, The Daycare was not ours, it did not belong to us. They answered to someone who sat in the office, they answered to the "owner." I remember the precise day that I came to this realization. I went to a private school just down the road run by a local church. Granny never drove in her life, so someone else would pick me up and take me back to "The Daycare." Now, usually this was a family member of mine: my dad, an aunt, or a cousin mostly. But, occasionally it would be the owner.

She was always nice, to me at least. She and her children were the only white people that I knew. On this day when she picked me up, I was waiting at school with a friend. When the friend saw that the white lady was there to pick me up, she looked startled. She quickly asked me, "Will, is that yo' auntie?" And I swiftly replied, "Nah, that's not my auntie, she's white." She signed me out and the car ride back to The Daycare was as quiet as the game of "heads up seven up" that I had played in school earlier that day.

When we got back to First Feats, she called Granny and my auntie Tina into her office. When they came out of the office, I was summoned. They reprimanded me for specifying the owner's whiteness in response to my friend's question and urged me to be grateful for her giving me a ride. I was careful not to ever offend the owner again. Sometimes, when I think about this story I wonder why I did not believe that I could have a white aunt.

As I have grown in my understanding of the history of race relations in my hometown and America overall, I have been able to identify a number of reasons. The first observation that I have been able to pinpoint is the fact that I grew up in a city that was and is segregated across racial lines: Birmingham, Alabama. Initially this was the result of Jim Crow laws, but now it exists as a product of "white flight." There is a physical, geographic feature that represents this phenomenon: Red Mountain. In our everyday lingo, if we ever say the phrase "over the mountain," we are referring to the majority-white suburbs that are situated on the opposite side of Red Mountain.

This kind of segregation shaped the kind of people that I was exposed to in all walks of life. The family members and friends that I lived, laughed, and cried with throughout life were Black. The people that I worshipped in church with on Sundays were Black. From what I saw and experienced, there was always a clear division in my mind: white people lived with other white people "over the mountain" and Black people lived with other Black people in the city.

There was nothing I ever witnessed that told me my aunt, let alone anyone in my family could be white. Now, for me, this story is indicative of something bigger in the city of

Birmingham and the rest of America's history: the disparity of wealth between African and Caucasian Americans. Throughout the history of America, white people have primarily existed as the "owners" and black people the "workers." This was the case on the plantations in the South where whites "owned" the black bodies that toiled the land for their profit. And it is the case today where, for instance, the largest fast-food corporations employ poor Black people today at a minimum wage rate.

At the inception of America's history and in the amended life, the roles have always seemed to be set. We know from a 2017 study by economist Thomas Piketty that 60% of wealth in America is inherited or passed down through family bloodlines. Today, much of the wealth is tied up in owning real estate, businesses, and access to greater education.

The Black people of Birmingham are largely descendants of slaves. Our ancestors never got their 40 acres and a mule. And it is also important to note that when Black people set out to build for themselves without white folk directly profiting, they were subjected to devastating domestic terrorism. We have seen the images of what happened to the Black Wall Street community in Tulsa, Oklahoma that was turning the tides for their families.

In Birmingham, we saw what happened at a place that we call "Dynamite Hill." When Black people there began to enter the middle class and move into such neighborhoods that were deemed to be intrinsically white, Black families had their homes bombed with dynamite to maintain white supremacy and segregation. When we tried to buy homes, our communities were redlined so we would not be able to attain home loans. Also, when we tried to integrate into the American economy as "free" Americans, those in power devised more complex ways to keep Black people subordinate not only socially, but economically.

Thinking of wealth and ownership within my community makes me think of something that one of my teachers told me when I was in the seventh grade. He said, "Look around man, the problem is that we don't own anything. We don't own the houses we live in. We don't own any of the places that we shop at. The people that own everything live 'over the mountain.' Make sure you own something in life William, it is very important." Then, I thought about how much I wished that my family owned The Daycare.

2

Sam Cooke

Half of my family consists of children and grandchildren of the Great Migration. In the mid-twentieth century, living in the Jim Crow South meant harsh segregation laws and limited economic opportunities. These living conditions lead millions of African Americans to flee these conditions for the North. Six of my great aunts and uncles were among these numbers. They all migrated to Detroit, Michigan where the booming economy surrounding the budding car manufacturing industry desperately needed workers.

I was 8 years old and living in Detroit at the time my sleep was interrupted by the most boisterous sound of a Black celebration I have ever heard. Why did I wake up to people joyfully screaming at the top of their lungs? Barack Obama had just been elected the 44th president of the United States. In the days, weeks, and months prior, my eyes could not miss the yard signs promoting the historic combo of Obama-Biden.

You could not miss the t-shirts displaying the slogan "Yes We Can;" and the many pieces of artwork that connected Obama to Dr. King, calling him the "Dream Realized." But, most of all, I remembered hearing Sam Cooke's voice over the radio singing, "It's been a long time coming, but I know a change gone come." And that, the representation and anticipation of a change coming for Black people in America, is what woke me up out of my sleep that evening.

The amended life in Detroit, the second Blackest city in the nation, was especially difficult at the time with an economic recession looming large. Living in the city, even at my youthful age, the suffering was palpable. I remember people being disgruntled at gas prices. I remember homeless people asking for spare change. I recall one night at a convenience store where a mother was begging fellow customers to buy food for her children. Fortunately, my mother was and is a nurse; therefore, she was usually on the giving side of things. With this being the scene in the city, some Black celebration for

Obama's election was more than warranted. The Black people in my home felt like he was going to change things—for the better—especially for us.

Not completely understanding the significance, I joined in on the screaming and high fives. I remember seeing him and his Black family on the screen and how much joy that put on my mother's face. I do not believe she went to sleep that night. I believe she was too full of absolute jubilation. I did, however, find my way back to my bed at the time, which was an air mattress in the living room. Growing up, I was accustomed to sleeping on pallets, pull out couches, and air mattresses. My time in Detroit was no different.

The next morning I woke up and got ready for school. I went to a charter school on the east side of Detroit called the Marvin L. Winans School of Fine Arts. We had a uniform where we had to wear burgundy pants, a white shirt, and burgundy tie. I always felt good with a fresh coat of Vaseline on my face and my school uniform on. At the Winans Academy, just as much impetus was put on the arts as academics. I took music, dance, art, and violin classes. But it wasn't until I took drama that I found what would turn out to be my childhood love.

I joined the drama club and stayed after school everyday to venture into characters with my friends. I remember this time of my life being so much fun. I would spend hours at home after drama club learning my lines. I would ask the drama teacher if I could improvise certain scenes. It was there that I felt the kind of joy and jubilation that I saw from my mother when she witnessed the election of a Black president after about 35 years of the amended life.

I have found that this is often the case for the amended life. We have to manufacture joy. Seldom does the news bring us jubilation. We produce ways of turning our pain into laughter and our heartache into happiness. The arts have always been instruments for the creation of joy, celebration, and comfort in the Black life. Sam Cooke soulfully singing that "a change is gonna come" comforts us just as much as Young Jeezy rapping "my president is black" affirms us. The images of the assassinated Martin Luther King Jr. alongside the 44th president of the United States signify the worthiness of the struggle for what Kiese Laymon calls Black Abundance.

3

Playing the Game

The white liberal must see that the Negro needs not only love but also justice. It is not enough to say, "We love Negroes, we have many Negro friends." They must demand justice for Negroes. Love that does not satisfy justice is no love at all." -MLK

In 1954, Brown v. The Board of Education made segregation illegal in public schools. This sparked the creation of private school associations across the south so that white parents could still have options to educate their children apart from Black children. These schools and institutions are commonly referred to as segregation academies by scholars. In 1966, the Alabama Independent School Association (AISA) was formed as the Alabama Private School Association, initially entailing 8 segregation academies. In 2008, Restoration Academy, an almost all Black school out of Fairfield, Alabama, joined the association. In the fall of 2010, I enrolled into Restoration Academy as a sixth grader.

I had no idea of the kind of history that I was stepping into. I was just a kid who had just moved back home from Detroit eager to learn. For the most part, learning is what I did. Unlike Winans Academy, there was very little focus on the arts. I remember googling auditions in Atlanta when we first moved back to Birmingham and begging my mom to take me. We never went. I had to find a new way to manufacture joy.

We produced joy on open fields of grass at the park playing football, making pencil beats on classroom desks, or cracking jokes at lunchroom tables. Nevertheless, nothing made me happier than seeing an A. I became obsessed with my studies and my grades. Although I could no longer venture into characters after school, I could explore social studies, math, and science. Therefore, being the best student I could be, became my focus. I didn't question much about what was going on at the time. I just laughed, had fun, and studied hard.

In the 7 and 8th grade, I began to notice confusing patterns.

Almost all of my teachers were white whilst all of my classmates were Black. We always had white "sponsors" and "donors" visit from "over the mountain" with food and stories about Jesus. Talking to a friend recently provided me some additional perspective on this phenomena. He said these visits always made him feel like he was an animal in a zoo. One might find this to be hyperbole but our experience lends credence to such a description. Zoo animals are thought to be exotic. They are taken out of their natural habitat and put on display for the pleasure and education of visitors.

At Restoration, Black students from the inner-city were marketed to a majority white donor base. On these visits a number of uncomfortable situations would arise for us students. Someone might seem fascinated by your hair and—even worse—ask to touch it. They would ask personal, invasive questions out of excessive curiosity. The cultural gap was palpable and created experiences that I would later learn are called "microaggressions."

Too often in the amended life, Black people's bodies and experiences are utilized to educate white people from "over the mountain." In schools, the books teach us white history and white customs. While doing so, these same books lack the kind of historical grounding that would bridge the gap of ignorance in these encounters. Therefore, white people—harboring a savior complex—are left feeling like they did a good deed after these engagements while Black folks feel like they were put on display.

The stories about Jesus are a big part of this. Once again, without some historical grounding one might think these thoughts to be far-fetched. On one hand, you have the historical truth that the Bible and Christianity were both used during slavery to state that Black people are inferior to white people and thus must be subservient to them. On the other hand, you have the historical fact of the life, death, and resurrection of Jesus Christ and its meaning for all people.

These things get muddled together when you have white people who believe themselves to be missionaries because they donate to a Christian school, bring food to Black kids from the inner-city, and tell them about Jesus. In all of this, there is the underlying belief that the problems of the inner-city stem from lack of belief in Jesus as opposed to 400 years of systemic oppression. Ultimately, events like these donor visits and luncheons served to absolve the white guilt from "over the mountain" more than they served to build up the Black students from Restoration Academy.

When I entered 9th grade, I had become accustomed to what we call "playing the game." I knew how to be a digestible Black man, that is someone who is adept at making white people feel less white. We call this code switching. You do this by not making them uncomfortable. You speak their language. You laugh at terribly bland jokes. And finally, you never tell them how you really feel. I would later learn how "playing the game" hurt some of my classmates who had no interest in doing so.

You see, to be put on display at Restoration was an everyday thing. But, in order to be given a stage at luncheons, to be given more opportunities to travel and network, one had to fit a certain mold. If you did not comply and fit into this mold, you were left behind. Even more, you were demonized by staff and administration. One of my friends who did not play the game was told by his math teacher that he wasn't good enough at math to be an engineer in front of the entire class. One would think that she was there to help him reach his dreams but she was there for herself. Today my friend is a successful engineer.

The intended audience largely determines the content in media, books, and life itself. This is why it is vitally important to choose the audience of your life wisely. Part of the frustration of being Black in America is feeling like you do not have the freedom to choose your audience. My love for academics and Jesus along with the ways that I emulated my white teachers led to white adulation. My classmates' love for themselves and our culture led to white agitation and confusion.

This led to Black culture being actively suppressed at Restoration in favor of white culture. Black male students had a length restriction on their hair that was one inch. This was considered the "professional" way to wear your hair. I now know that "professional" is just another way of saying "palatable" or "acceptable" to white folks. And sadly, this length restriction was not enforced on the few white male students that attended the school.

I will never forget that we were banned from playing spades at lunch because of how spirited we competed and slapped the cards on the table. The Black Abundance was too much for them to handle. I was once told by a bible teacher that gospel music, created in the Black American tradition, was no match for Christian contemporary music.

While our culture was being suppressed at school in Fairfield, our sports teams were being subjected to utter racism while traveling. During my 11th grade year, our basketball team traveled to Phenix City, Alabama to play a team called Glenwood, now in the aforementioned AISA. During the layup line, the young men were repeatedly called "niggers." The one white gentleman on our team was called a "nigger lover." This was 2016 in the middle of the Kaepernick protests and the Trump campaign.

While many continue to argue that sports brings people together and we live in a post racial society, our players were being called "niggers" just like Jackie Robinson was being called a "nigger" at the plate during the Jim Crow era. Unsurprisingly, that night ended with Restoration forfeiting as our head coach was disrespected by a referee and the team had to evacuate the scene. Even though our players could return home that night, they will never be able to erase the memories of the dehumanization they experienced that night.

To experience such humiliation one evening and return to school the next day to hear your math teacher lobby for Donald Trump to be president, has to be the most befuddling thing for a 16 or 17 year old Black man. I remember the day as it was yesterday. I jokingly told a friend that "I would take 4 more years of Obama before I take Trump as president." My math teacher interjected and exclaimed, "Oh no! I would rather have Trump than Obama!" We would spend subsequent days, weeks, and months arguing about the impending presidential election.

In a world where I thought image and fitting the mold was king, the man who was recorded saying in regards to women that you can just grab them by the pu**y was the prime candidate for white evangelicals. This was the turning point for me. This is where I first learned that being white was more important than being Christian or morally upright.

During my senior year, my friends and I were tired of the subjugation. We wanted something for us where we could be real with one another, somewhere at school where we did not have to "play the game." Out of this yearning, something called "The Focus" was born. The Focus was a bi-weekly hour of time that our senior class hosted before school where we would talk about topics affecting our lives.

We touched on things like not fitting the mold, fatherlessness, the culture, and race. November 9, 2016 was the day after Trump was elected and we had an iteration of The Focus. This was our most attended session as people, not fully understanding what had just happened, were devastated. We spent the hour that morning mourning and comforting one another.

In the following weeks and months, my friends and I were applying to colleges. I knew from a very young age that I wanted to go to college. I thought it was the only route to a better life. My goal was always to get rich and someday take care of my family. I now know that college is not the only route to financial success. Alternatives like obtaining a trade or jumping right into entrepreneurship are worthy as well. I also am aware that being financially free does not unequivocally lead to a healthy, fruitful life.

Nonetheless, whether it was junior college or a four year institution, everyone at Restoration was encouraged to go to college. However, the level of support that you got in making that a reality relied on how well you "played the game" and what college you wanted to attend. Students who wanted to go to HBCUs—historically Black colleges and universities—were actively discouraged not to do so. One friend of mine who matriculated at Morehouse College in Atlanta, Georgia was told that the school was a party school. There was the terrible trope that the Black experience at HBCUs somehow does not extend to academics. We were encouraged to apply everywhere but they wanted to see us land at PWIs—predominantly white institutions.

Luckily my class had a science teacher who was a champion for HBCUs. His professionalism, swagger, relationship building ability, and more convinced almost a third of my class that an HBCU was the right place for them. 5 of my 17 classmates had their eyes set on following in his footsteps to Alabama A&M, affectionately called "The Hill." I had my eyes set on Tuskegee for a while but was quickly redirected to the alma mater of other school leaders who were the principal and executive director at the time. This institution was located about 40 miles west of Chicago, Illinois and called Wheaton College.

From my sophomore year of high school onward we had a recruiter come visit from Wheaton College. The recruiter was a tall, Black man from Chicago with dreadlocks. Now, the first two years I saw him and heard the story of the college, I was not sold. But my senior year was different. I listened to what he had to say. I also must admit that despite knowing that the college was a PWI, I was impressed that the recruiter was a Black man and also an alum. This said to me that there was a place for me there. That's another thing I have learned in the amended life: We are not a monolith.

Too often our characters and experiences get lumped into a box. Just because he could survive, thrive, and even work at Wheaton as a Black man did not mean I could, however, I did get the opportunity to see for myself. In March 2017, I got the opportunity to visit Wheaton for something that they call the Wheaton Connection.

This connection experience was either a huge coincidence or extremely well positioned to recruit someone like me. In chapel that day, the speaker was the Black chaplain. The music was led by the gospel choir and they sang songs that my mom and I were accustomed to at our own church. The food was delicious. We finished off the trip with a visit to downtown Chicago where we had deep dish pizza and enjoyed a nice architectural tour of downtown on a boat. Finally, I also received a full-ride scholarship.

After this trip, my mom and I both were convinced that this was the place for me. We had no further questions. My friend who eventually went to Morehouse and his parents also went on this trip. He and his parents had a multitude of questions. The one that stood out the most to me was asked by his mom:

"How will he find his Black queen here?" I don't remember how that question was answered but in hindsight it was very valid. I, for one, was not even interested in dating at the time, but she had noticed the paucity of Black students much more keenly than I or my mom did.

Once we returned, I started telling everyone I was going to Wheaton and on April 9, 2017, I signed my scholarship. At that moment, I was happy to be signing up to continue my white evangelical education, to continue "playing the game."

4

The Nod

Why God, Why God do I gotta suffer? Every stone thrown at you resting at my feet." – Kendrick Lamar

"Cop another bag and smoke today." – J Cole

Black people comprise 12% of the population in the United States of America. At Wheaton College in Illinois, roughly 2% of the student body is Black. If you spend some considerable time on Wheaton's campus, you will find that about half of that 2% actually identifies with their Black heritage in a meaningful way. Stepping foot on this campus was an absolute culture shock. I was used to curious looks from white people who I don't know, however, I always found comfort in the acknowledgment of my personhood from other Black people that I don't know. Usually this came in the form of a simple head nod, or even better, a warm "hey how are you." This always made me feel connected in some strange way to the 12% of Black people in this country.

Thus, one thing I thought I could be sure of at Wheaton was that there would be a strong connection within this 2%. But, as I walked the campus, I noticed that some Black people would not acknowledge my personhood. They wouldn't do the nod. They would not speak. Some would purposely look away. I was so confused. So, after a week of orientation activities, I did some research. I found out that there was a Black Student Union on campus called the William Osborne Society, named after the first Black man to graduate from Wheaton.

I was delighted to find an email from the president of the organization. I contacted her immediately and asked if we could meet up and talk. We met and she embraced me like I was accustomed to being embraced. At the end of our talk, she took me to what we called the OMD, which stands for the Office of Multicultural Development.

As we walked in there, I saw more embraces that I was familiar with. A head nod here. A dap there. I thought to myself "so this is where the Black people talk to each other." I was correct. The OMD was where the Black people who wanted to identify with their heritage during college convened. This space was not only for Black people. As I would soon learn, multicultural was code word for not white. But, it also was not just for multicultural people. Everyone at Wheaton was encouraged to visit the OMD.

The space was not particularly big or anything but we made it work. The OMD was the only place on campus where Black people gave white people curious looks when they walked in. All of this was completely different than what I was used to in Birmingham and Detroit. Though I was used to playing the game, my blackness was never confined to a space.

As eerie as this was, I and other Black first-year students quickly adapted. For about 3-4 hours of classes a day we code switched as 2 percenters. When classes concluded, you would see a steady stream of Black people making our way to the OMD where we could exhale and be acknowledged. I spent too much of my first two semesters holding my breath. I was so excited early on that I found myself wrapped up in multiple extracurricular activities where I was the only Black person. The amended life can be utterly exhausting when striving for excellence and sometimes means deprivation of affirmation. Luckily, because of the OMD, I did not have too much trouble making friends.

The friends I met in the early stages of my Wheaton career were well-seasoned vets in the amended life on campus. Many were already exhausted from holding their collective breath for years. To cope they exhaled ounces of weed, consumed liters of liquor, and listened to hours of music. Unbeknownst to me, I would soon be exhausted. Nevertheless, my first-year was a watchful, listening year. I learned so much about the culture of the campus and why the 2% was not strong.

Amongst other things, I learned that the Black players on the football team were discouraged from engaging meaningfully with other Black people on campus. I learned that some Black staff were not supportive of the students on the Black Student Union and that there were countless racial incidents on campus that were sorely mishandled by the college's administration.

After a year of watching and listening, I thought, "Whew, what have I gotten myself into?" I was a business major. In life I always enjoyed writing the script and pulling the strings behind the scenes. I knew going into college that this was the major for me. But, like many other Black students, I had to begin to equip myself for an environment that at any moment could dehumanize you. This is a staple in the amended life. We have to supplement our conventional education in order to uncover the truth and get a better understanding of the history we are facing.

We equipped ourselves with books from authors like James Baldwin, Kiese Laymon, Toni Morrison, and Jesmyn Ward, just to name a few. These books, along with the Bible, were like our sword and shield. We shielded ourselves from alienation by leaning into Black art and fellowship. We fended for ourselves with the truth of Scripture when white supremacy seemed to reign supreme on campus.

All of this fending and advocating for myself as a young adult and student was not what I was expecting out of college. I was expecting "pure D" fun, friends, and personal development. I got all of those things but it wasn't "pure D." I had to go through hardships like depression, loneliness, and anxiety to achieve these things. Now, there is the concept that one does not accomplish anything worthwhile without suffering, however, there is a difference between growing pains and institutionally imposed deprivation.

After feeling deprived for most of my first year at Wheaton, I decided to completely devote all of my time and efforts outside of the classroom to the OMD. The OMD was overflowing with talent but severely under-resourced. The mission that it was given is two-fold, "to promote the flourishing of students of diverse backgrounds and provide opportunities for the majority students to engage with issues of diversity." In my experience, these two things could not be accomplished under the guise of one roof. While attempting to promote the flourishing of Black students on campus there would be backlash from majority students.

While attempting to provide opportunities for majority students to engage with diversity, the culture and bodies of Black students were masqueraded for the benefit of white students. In all of this, general diversity talk, true equity and inclusion was nonexistent. Where equity and inclusion are nonexistent in the amended life, Black people are left to pick up the pieces. Though the pieces were many, we always fought to be dignified on a campus that we believed was just as much ours as majority students.

During my sophomore year, I joined the cabinet of the Black Student Union as the "Brotherhood Coordinator." This meant that I was primarily tasked with creating community for Black men on campus. This would prove to be difficult as many Black men on campus were among the number who would not "do the nod." Nevertheless, I attempted to manufacture joy with game nights, prayer gatherings, and outings. Most of my time was spent trying to reach out to those Black men who would not step foot in the OMD or any Black Student Union event.

Something told me that they were suffering from deprivation too, even if it was a little different. This also was the year that the cabinet had the lofty goal of going on a civil rights retreat through the South over Spring Break. We spent hours outside of our school work educating ourselves, putting together an itinerary, and planning this trip.

The retreat took 30 students through four pivotal cities from the civil rights movement: Birmingham, Selma, Montgomery, and Atlanta. Unlike a traditional Spring Break, this trip was not fun or relaxing. As I mentioned in the preface, we were confronted head-on with not only America's history but also that history's effect on today. We left the South completely displeased with the two-fold mission of the OMD, and thus utterly displeased with much of our college experience up to that point.

In the aftermath of this trip, I was set on transferring out of Wheaton. But, there is the notion that I was in too deep. I didn't really want to leave my friends behind and try and make new ones in a new environment. I had already adapted to Wheaton; had confined my blackness to a space; and had found ways to cope with my suffering. I was depressed. I was angry. I was befuddled. For the first time in my life I felt trapped.

I carried all these feelings into my junior year at Wheaton. I was still ensconced in the OMD. To cope with all the anger, depression, and suffering I had delved deeper into my coping mechanisms. I exhaled more ounces of weed. I drank more liters of liquor. And I listened to hours upon hours of music.

Then, after a night of the all familiar trio, an email appeared in my inbox from the college that essentially said, "Due to the spread of a contagious virus, we need you to pack up all your stuff and leave immediately." In the moment I read these words, I honestly was burnt out on campus and running on fumes, therefore, part of me was grateful for an out. I exhaled, having no idea of what carnage the COVID-19 pandemic would eventually bring.

5

They Must See Roaches

At the beginning of the pandemic, I needed to rest mentally, physically, and emotionally. Usually being home in Birmingham, Alabama does that for me. The utter disregard for Black life that the pandemic unleashed did not grant rest of any kind. News, stories and video footage of racist murders collectively exhausted me. Most notably, the killings of Breonna Taylor, Ahmaud Arbery, and George Floyd caused even more anger, depression, and grief.

The nature of the pandemic made these realities inescapable. There was nowhere to go, nothing to do, but sit and contemplate life. I began to write, specifically journal. I started documenting the pain I was feeling. After the George Floyd news and footage came out, I wrote the following poem entitled "They Must See Roaches."

"You ever stepped on a roach before?

You ever feel that brittle frame crack beneath the weight of your shoe? And wipe the guts up from the floor?

You ever think twice about it?

"Roaches nasty"

"Roaches make my skin crawl"

"Uh uh, kill that roach before he have my house infested" "Get my shoe, I'm bout to kill this roach"

You ever walk home from the store? You ever been on a run?

You ever hustle to feed your family? You ever sleep in your own bed?

You ever think it could be your last time?

"I was afraid. He was threatening me."

"This isn't his neighborhood, he doesn't belong here."

"He fit the description."

"He whistled at a white woman."

"I'm going to call the police."

Oh, the way they step on us

> With shoes, with dogs, with guns, with knees, with elbows, with nightsticks
> And don't think twice
> Stepped on George Floyd
> Stepped on Ahmaud Arbery
> Stepped on Breonna Taylor
> Stepped on Eric Garner
> Stepped on Emmitt Till
> Stepped on so many more
>
> They must see roaches, the way they step on us." – **Will Creagh**

These were the only words I could muster up at the time. These words are relevant as I write this chapter in 2023 after the Tyre Nichols footage and news has been released.

In 2020, the only words that Wheaton College administration could muster up—at least initially—was something along the lines of "let's pray for our country." They did not mention the names of those brutalized. They did not name what killed them. They did not even make at least a verbal commitment to institutional equity and inclusion like many leading organizations and corporations at the time. This infuriated me and my peers; therefore, we drafted a letter to the administration and flooded their inbox with it. The letter we sent is as follows:

"Dear Wheaton College, Senior Administrative Cabinet, I have received your emails, messages, and videos expressing your support and prayers during the circumstances surrounding the COVID-19 global pandemic. I believe it is important for the college administration to explicitly communicate its prayers to the campus. For racialized minorities attending Wheaton (and especially Black people), the request for prayer should be more than the mental strain that stems from having to abruptly transition to remote learning; more than the vocational anxiety that many students are experiencing due to lost internships; and more than the financial strain that this pandemic has put on Wheaton college families.

The call for prayer that the campus community received tonight was incredibly insufficient and noticeably overdue. It also failed to mention the names of those unjustly murdered. The college administration has to align its call for prayers with efforts to specifically address the unique challenges that white-supremacy, and police brutality, and the racial disparities within COVID-19 has posed for multicultural Wheaton students. I ask, as this letter addresses, that the college formulate an official statement in regard to the implications of the following events.

The American sickness that we see affecting racial minorities at Wheaton is the deadly manifestations of systemic injustice on unarmed Black men and women across the country. Blanket statements that do not address the unique trauma and experiences associated with this–which are often used to mask White supremacist ideologies–can not suffice for a Christian community that strives to "weep with those who weep and mourn with those who mourn" (Romans 12:15). Recently, national leadership referred to protestors of the unlawful murders as "thugs."

These comments clearly represent a racially motivated response to the public displeasure with repeated incidents of innocent Black people dying. These comments came after armed white protesters, who were displeased with government restrictions meant to keep the public safe from infection, were called "very good people." Wheaton College proudly boasts the institution's abolitionists roots and it's early leaders' stances on slavery. I, a student who loves the community deeply, want to be sure that the college understands and confronts the modern-day manifestations of slavery. Our God is not merely a God of justice, our God is justice.

An attempt to wholly educate students to serve Christ and His Kingdom falls short if the institution does not also educate about the demonic racial ills of this society. It has been months since the murder of Ahmaud Arbery, weeks since the murder of Breonna Taylor, and days since the murder of George Floyd. Still, the student body has yet to receive an official statement on behalf of the college. Other institutions of higher learning, companies, and organizations have already taken this important initiative.

I urge that as an institution we commit to standing and supporting our Black brothers and sisters during this time of grief. This means explicitly condemning the unjust, unholy killing of unarmed Black men and women in unison with our prayers. The institution should do this in accordance with its very own Diversity Commitment which says that it will "recognize and lament the sinful and self-serving use of power that divides the body of Christ, while supporting those in our community who have been disadvantaged or oppressed."

After hundreds of emails went out from students, alumni, and

Wheaton community members, the college released a formal statement which read:

"Dear Campus Community,

We all are witnesses to the egregious and senseless violence that recently claimed the lives of Breonna Taylor, Ahmaud Arbery, and George Floyd. Their deaths speak to the enduring presence of systematic and institutional racism within our society. As a community, we are deeply distressed by violent acts that have persisted in our country for more than four centuries.

As Christ followers, we denounce systemic racism and police brutality against any racial or ethnic group. Today especially our hearts are filled with pain for the inhumane treatment of our brothers and sisters in the African American community. We stand united with African American students, faculty, and staff who are all deeply affected by these ongoing acts of racial violence and other sinful injustices, often on a daily basis.

Wheaton College believes that the physical, emotional and spiritual well-being of our students, faculty and staff within the African American community is essential for learning and thriving. Therefore, we are also committed to identifying and addressing policies and systems in our own institution that hinder access and success of members who belong to marginalized and oppressed groups. In order to have the impact on the world that God is calling us to have, we are resolved to think and act in ways that create a more loving, equitable, and just community.

Wheaton College pursues a biblical commitment to respect and love all people as equal image-bearers of Jesus Christ. This is mandated by Scripture, promised in our Community Covenant, and detailed in our Christ-Centered Diversity Commitment. As part of this commitment, we plan in coming days to curate a conversation featuring administrators, faculty, and staff on Christian responses to racial violence. To the members of our community belonging to the African diaspora, please know that you have our love, support, and concern. We pray for God's grace and protection on you and your families during this difficult time in our nation's history.

Please remember that this summer, as always, you can receive counseling and support through the Office of Multicultural Development, the Office of Student Care Services, the Counseling Center, the Title IX Coordinator, the Office of Intercultural Engagement, and the Chaplain's Office.

In keeping with our calling to pray, we intercede specifically for God's comfort for the families of those who have lost their loved ones, for God's healing and sanctifying work in our world, and for God's protection and guidance for our campus community." To put it in layman's terms, talk is cheap.

Wheaton College's hypocrisy serves as a microcosm of the hypocrisy of this nation. The United States has yet to live up to its founding principles of liberty and justice for all. Instead, it has feasted upon its founding sin, which is widespread institutional oppression.

6

Stigma

Coming to this realization—that is becoming conscious of racism—as a young Black man with dreams was not easy for me. As James Baldwin astutely said, "To be Black and relatively conscious in this country is to almost be in a constant state of rage." I was confused. I was angry. I was depressed. I continued to use coping mechanisms. It was not helping, it was only keeping me afloat.

In the fall of 2020 during an election year, I returned to Wheaton's campus as a senior at my own volition. I missed my friends. I did not want to do virtual classes. And yes, I was still entrenched in the OMD. That semester I was slated to serve as the Vice President of the Black Student Union. In all honesty,

I was not in a good place to serve in this capacity or even be taking classes at the time. But, I was afraid of looking like a failure or letting my friends down. I was still trapped and once again holding my proverbial breath on Wheaton's campus.

When I returned to my campus home one day my neighbors greeted me and my Black roommates with a "Blue Lives Matter" flag. Classmates taunted me and friends with Trump paraphernalia. I was seething all the time. I began to double my consumption of weed, alcohol, and music to cope. This semester it was not even keeping me afloat. I became more and more mentally ill by the day.

I had begun to suffer from insomnia, increased heartbeat, anxiety, and severe depression. Living with depression is like having a nagging, leaky tire and sometimes waking up to a flat. I began to have sporadic fits of uncontrollable crying. I was not well and I knew it. I could not do schoolwork in this condition. I reached out to the Student Care office to get a letter of support and missed classes for a week. During that week I went into the city of Chicago with friends who had graduated already for support. Without them I would not have made it through the Fall 2020 semester.

Once the semester was over, I packed all my belongings

again knowing I needed a break. My friends were worried and curious as to why I packed everything when we had another semester to go. I knew deep down that if I was going to complete the Spring 2021 semester, then it would have to be virtual. I drove the ten and a half hours home down I-65 on fumes.

When I returned home from Wheaton, the demons did not seem to be left behind. I was still suffering from anxiety, insomnia, and depression. Most of my time in December 2020 was spent in dark rooms with dark liquor, in cars with marijuana and music, and in my own head.

Then came the January 6th attack on the capitol. I was not only enraged but I was genuinely afraid. I began to spiral. By the end of January 2021, I had not slept in days, was trying to withdraw from weed, and experiencing a total mental breakdown. Not only was I confused, angry, and depressed, now all of a sudden I was extremely paranoid, incredibly anxious, and terribly afraid.

I spent the next two months in a mental institution. Once I got out of the hospital, I began doing therapy weekly. I started to work through the 21 years of traumatic experiences that landed me in a mental hospital for 8 weeks. In the amended life,

Black mental health is overlooked for Black survival. There is also the truth that our communities historically have not had access to resources like the necessary healthcare and finances to care for ourselves mentally.

With that being said, we are not surviving by not caring for ourselves mentally and emotionally, we are only compounding trauma. I encourage anyone reading, especially young Black people, to seek help immediately before things get out of your control. Be careful not to become reliant on coping mechanisms.

I personally have found journaling helpful in fighting my mental demons. I also have found it important to lean on the people who love and care for me. I used to say I hate high maintenance people until I myself needed a great deal of maintenance. I am so grateful I had friends and family who loved this high maintenance person. In life, sometimes all of the lights on the dashboard are on. Do not keep trying to drive. It is exhausting trying to fend for yourself all the time. When possible, choose spaces that already love you, where you do not feel the need to earn your God-given dignity. Care for yourselves the way this world does not, my friends.

7

Epilogue:

I know it must be strange to read the memoir of a 23 year old. Trust me, I have felt many times during this process that maybe I should not be writing this. But this is a more focused memoir, particularly about my journey to racial consciousness. I figured my story had something to offer to the world so I went for it.

I talk a lot about the amended life in this book. This is a concept I prefaced the book with to provide a framework for looking at Black life in the United States. The amended life is about how flawed systems, institutions, and circumstances collectively affect the Black body and mind. At the young age of 21, the amended life had exhausted my Black body and mind to the point of hospitalization.

I started with this question: What does it mean for your life, your humanity, your livelihood to rest upon a constitutional amendment? I also stated that as I surveyed America's history with Black life I am befuddled. It is clear to me that the United States does not love Black life. What is confusing is why lie so much and say that you do? That is what the amended life is built on: lies.

In writing, Black people have citizenship; in writing, Black people have voting rights; in writing, Black people have dignity. In practice, Black people enjoy none of these privileges fully. It seems to me that the amendments are just another ploy for American exceptionalism. The United States does not seem reticent at all to live up to any of its promises to its people except for those who are white.

Next, I shared the story of how I did not think anyone in my family could be white as a child. At six years old in 2005, Birmingham had instilled this idea of segregation in my mind. At twenty-three years old in 2023, I have seen many manifestations of integration. My all Black high school is operated by a white administration and staff. My alma mater is a predominantly white institution. But, what I have also seen in these spaces is the manifestation of white supremacy, white ignorance, and white guilt.

White supremacy is unwelded power that systematically oppresses all that refuse to comply with its laws and customs. White ignorance serves to uphold white supremacy by actively romanticizing and falsifying history. James Baldwin addressed how these two operate together saying that "ignorance allied with power is the most ferocious enemy justice can have." All of this gives way for white guilt. White guilt will do anything to absolve itself but relinquish white power.

In Chapter 3, I wrote about how white guilt operated at my high school. I fear this is the chapter I will have to answer for the most. First and foremost, this idea that Black students should just be grateful for the outcomes that white institutions produce and ignore the trauma they experienced along the way is dehumanizing. Being grateful for the outcome that an institution helped you achieve does not mean it did not cause you a good deal of harm and trauma. I am grateful for the Restoration Academy allowing me to travel, letting me earn a diploma, and helping me earn a scholarship to college.

However, the experiences I wrote about in chapter 3 are nothing to be grateful for.

In Chapter 4, I wrote about my time at Wheaton. My Wheaton education—inside and outside the classroom—really opened my eyes to a lot of the thinking in this book. Wheaton was where I was exposed to Black thought and writers. This was also the place where I made lifelong friendships and memories that I will cherish forever. Simultaneously, this is the place that I and many others met despair. And once again, this is nothing to be grateful for.

In Chapter 5, I wrote about the evil of police brutality and how it affected me mentally. I poetically said they must see roaches when they see Black people. In today's digital age, we witnessed Rodney King; we witnessed George Floyd; we witnessed Tyre Nichols. It is not normal or ok to watch another human get murdered on a screen like they are nothing. Even more, it is not acceptable for every one of these individuals to look just like you. It is enraging. Once again, this is nothing to be grateful for.

Lastly, I wrote about the amended life's effect on my mental health. There are different types of traumas. I am the furthest thing from a psychiatrist or mental health professional.

But, of all the Black people that I met in the hospital, I would say almost all of them were suffering from some kind of racial trauma at the time. Racial trauma was not my official diagnosis, but it is real. Ask any Black person of some consciousness and they will tell you so. I believe that we all, regardless of race or ethnicity, are suffering from the evils of white supremacy—of history—in one way or another. The question remains will we face this history with courage as Maya Angelou suggests, or will we continue to turn away?

About the Author

"Amended follows Will Creagh, a young African-American man from Birmingham, AL and Detroit, MI, throughout his childhood and into his college years. The book is centered around the question: "What does it mean for your livelihood to rest upon a Constitutional amendment?" Like other

American youth, Will grew up in schools. He reflects on this journey from childhood to adulthood through the lens of his racial experiences in education. He is particularly interested in how Black America encounters history and it's affect on the Black life and mind. In the book, the 25 year-old author and social entrepreneur discusses personal struggles with mental health and substance abuse. Will wants better outcomes for Black youth and believes that the question he poses in these pages should be explored for answers."

Connect with Will on social media:
Instagram – @big.time.will
Facebook – Will Creagh

www.ingramcontent.com/pod-product-compliance
Lightning Source LLC
Chambersburg PA
CBHW071915070526
44583CB00016B/2005